Library of
Davidson College

Futures Markets: An Overview of the AEI Studies

Futures Markets: An Overview of the AEI Studies

Philip McBride Johnson

American Enterprise Institute for Public Policy Research
Washington, D.C.

Philip McBride Johnson is a partner in the law firm of Skadden, Arps, Slate, Meagher & Flom in New York, author of the two-volume legal treatise *Commodities Regulation* (Little, Brown and Company, 1982), and former chairman of the Commodity Futures Trading Commission.

Library of Congress Cataloging-in-Publication Data

Johnson, Philip McBride.
  Futures markets.

  (AEI Studies ; 439)
  Bibliography: p.
  1. Commodity exchanges—United States. I. American Enterprise Institute for Public Policy Research.
II. Title. III. Series.
HG6049.J64 1986   332.63'28'0973   86-1028
ISBN 0-8447-3597-3

1 3 5 7 9 10 8 6 4 2

AEI Studies 439

© 1986 by the American Enterprise Institute for Public Policy Research, Washington, D.C. All rights reserved. No part of this publication may be used or reproduced in any manner whatsoever without permission in writing from the American Enterprise Institute except in the case of brief quotations embodied in news articles, critical articles, or reviews. The views expressed in the publications of the American Enterprise Institute are those of the authors and do not necessarily reflect the views of the staff, advisory panels, officers, or trustees of AEI.

"American Enterprise Institute" and are registered service marks of the American Enterprise Institute for Public Policy Research.

Printed in the United States of America

Contents

Foreword *William J. Baroody, Jr.*		vii
Preface *Marvin H. Kosters*		ix
Introduction		1
1	Cash Settlement	3
2	New Products	6
3	The "Level Playing Field"	12
4	The Margin Debate	15
5	The Nonprice Benefits of Futures	17
6	Futures in Live or Perishable Commodities	19
7	The Dynamics of Regulation	21
8	Final Note: Playing to Strength	22
	Notes	27

The **American Enterprise Institute for Public Policy Research**, established in 1943, is a nonpartisan, nonprofit research and educational organization supported by foundations, corporations, and the public at large. Its purpose is to assist policy makers, scholars, business men and women, the press, and the public by providing objective analysis of national and international issues. Views expressed in the institute's publications are those of the authors and do not necessarily reflect the views of the staff, advisory panels, officers, or trustees of AEI.

Council of Academic Advisers

Paul W. McCracken, *Chairman, Edmund Ezra Day University Professor of Business Administration, University of Michigan*

Donald C. Hellmann, *Professor of Political Science and International Studies, University of Washington*

D. Gale Johnson, *Eliakim Hastings Moore Distinguished Service Professor of Economics and Chairman, Department of Economics, University of Chicago*

Robert A. Nisbet, *Adjunct Scholar, American Enterprise Institute*

Herbert Stein, *A. Willis Robertson Professor of Economics Emeritus, University of Virginia*

Murray L. Weidenbaum, *Mallinckrodt Distinguished University Professor and Director, Center for the Study of American Business, Washington University*

James Q. Wilson, *Henry Lee Shattuck Professor of Government, Harvard University*

Executive Committee

Richard B. Madden,
  Chairman of the Board
Willard C. Butcher, *Vice Chairman*
William J. Baroody, Jr., *President*

John J. Creedon
Richard M. Morrow
Paul F. Oreffice
Richard D. Wood

Robert J. Pranger,
  Vice President, External Affairs
Thomas F. Johnson,
  Director, Economic Policy Studies
Howard R. Penniman,
  Director, Political Processes Studies

James W. Abellera, *Acting Director, International Studies*
William A. Schambra,
  Director, Social Policy Studies
Edward Styles,
  Director of Publications

Periodicals

AEI Economist, Herbert Stein, *Ed.*

AEI Foreign Policy and Defense Review,
  Evron M. Kirkpatrick,
  Robert J. Pranger, and
  Harold H. Saunders, *Eds.*

Public Opinion, Seymour Martin
  Lipset and Ben J. Wattenberg, *Co-Eds.*,
  Everett Carll Ladd, *Sr. Ed.*,
  Karlyn H. Keene, *Mng. Ed.*

Regulation: AEI Journal on Government and Society

Foreword

The American Enterprise Institute was led by several developments to conduct a series of studies on the economics and regulation of futures markets. The dramatic growth in the number and kinds of contracts traded on futures markets raised new concerns about their role. After its periodic review and revision of the legislative framework for futures trading in 1982, the Congress mandated studies by federal government agencies of various issues. And in view of AEI's continuing program of research and dissemination of regulatory policy analyses on timely issues, we received encouragement from several sources in industry and government to examine futures markets and their regulation.

This small overview volume by Philip McBride Johnson draws on the analyses in the background studies carried out under the AEI project to show how each addresses important elements of an interrelated set of policies, arrangements, and commercial and financial practices that together constitute the workings of futures markets. He sketches out the main themes of the studies, highlights their significance for policies and practices in the futures industry, and puts forward some of his own ideas about new roles and applications for futures.

The studies that form the basis for this overview were published as a part of AEI's project on the Economics and Regulation of Futures Markets. They are *Futures Markets: Their Economic Role* and *Futures Markets: Regulatory Issues*, edited by Anne E. Peck, who served as project director. Futures markets and their relation to other markets are also analyzed in an earlier AEI publication, *A Treatise on Markets: Spot, Futures, and Options*, by Joseph M. Burns.

These studies are intended to contribute to a better understanding of the economic role of futures markets and the role of regulation so as to improve public policy formation in this important area. The project on futures markets was carried out under the auspices of AEI's Center for the Study of Government Regulation, directed by Marvin H. Kosters. The government regulation studies program at AEI has addressed a wide range of issues concerning the appropriate role of government. These studies by leading scholars and practitioners in their fields analyze the contribution that efficiently functioning futures markets make to achieving broader economic goals. They are particularly relevant in the current climate of public concern about meeting capital investment needs and about appropriate regulatory structures for financial services markets.

WILLIAM J. BAROODY, JR.
President
American Enterprise Institute

Preface

In highlighting the main themes and policy implications of a series of AEI studies on futures markets, this overview draws on the studies themselves and on the author's experience as a legal practitioner on financial and futures market issues and as a former chairman of the Commodity Futures Trading Commission. It presents important perspectives on how new developments give rise to new policy concerns and how careful analyses of experience provide insights relevant to current public policy concerns.

The AEI project on the Economics and Regulation of Futures Markets under which these studies were carried out was stimulated by several related developments. There has, first of all, been a dramatic surge in futures market trading in recent years. The number of contracts traded in traditional agricultural commodities and metals increased greatly in the more volatile and inflationary climate of the 1970s. The introduction and phenomenal growth of trading in financial futures contracts was even more significant. Between 1970 and 1985 futures trading volume increased more than tenfold, and by 1985 financial futures accounted for 60 percent of total trading.

The framework for futures market regulation was also changed, first with the establishment of the Commodity Futures Trading Commission and subsequently with the Futures Trading acts of 1978 and 1982. The four-year sunset provision in the 1974 legislation, together with the government studies mandated by the 1982 act, ensured that several important issues would be on the national policy agenda for the next round of reauthorization.

The remarkable expansion of trading in financial futures has meant a more important and pervasive economy-wide role for futures markets. This expanded role has raised new issues, issues that deserve analysis by recognized scholars in the private sector as well as by experts in government. Like most markets, futures markets usually perform their essential economic functions without drawing much public attention. But major new developments in patterns of use or in prices often attract the attention of the public and of government.

The implications of financial futures trading and the issues that arose in connection with such developments as the emergence of trading in stock index futures and options on futures contracts were not well understood. In the congressional hearings before the Commodity Futures Trading Commission (CFTC) was reauthorized, questions were raised about the growing array of derivative financial instruments trading on futures markets, the economic purposes they served, the extent to which they might be competitive with the well-established securities markets, and possible conflicts or overlap in the regulatory systems administered by different federal government agencies. Congressional concerns about these issues led to requests in the Futures Trading Act of 1982 for studies to be conducted by federal government agencies.

The Federal Reserve Board (FRB), the Securities and Exchange Commission (SEC), and the CFTC were directed by the act to carry out a joint study of the economic purposes of futures and options markets, to consider their effects on capital formation, and to evaluate the adequacy of their regulation. The CFTC was directed to examine the implications of trading on futures markets by individuals possessing material nonpublic information. Finally, the FRB had announced a study to review federal policy on margin regulation. These three federal studies were under way by the spring of 1983.

In view of this concentration of government interest, the American Enterprise Institute initiated a project that would sponsor additional research by leading scholars outside government to contribute to a better understanding in the Washington policy community of futures markets, their economic roles, and related regulatory issues. The background studies arising from this research effort are published in two volumes: *Futures Markets: Their Economic Role* and *Futures Markets: Regulatory Issues*. Lists of the studies in these two volumes and a list of the contributors are printed at the back of this book.

The studies in the *Economic Role* volume assess the economic contributions of futures and options markets by drawing on evidence from the long history of futures trading in largely agricultural products, by examining the newer financial futures and options markets, and by analyzing implications for capital formation. The studies analyze how trading in financial futures instruments facilitates the management of interest rate and security price risks, thereby reducing the cost of capital and increasing incentives to invest in productive assets. Finally, the studies discuss the key underlying economic differences between futures and securities markets, which provide the basis for the different forms and methods of regulation in these markets.

The studies in the *Regulatory Issues* volume address market practices, institutions, or participants and associated regulatory concerns. Each of the current congressional concerns has a historical context. Some concerns, such as the regulation of futures margins, have long histories of congressional debate. Other issues, such as trading floor practices, arise in a new context because different, but related, financial instruments are traded under separate regulatory systems. The issues discussed are trading floor practices, the role and adequacy of margins, characteristics of small public traders, cash settlement of contracts, and livestock futures.

Taken together, these AEI studies show that careful analysis of futures markets and instruments and of industry practices is essential for understanding their economic contribution. They indicate that a complex set of institutional arrangements, commercial and financial practices, privately administered rules, and federal regulations has evolved in a highly competitive market environment to foster efficient and financially secure trading. Finally, the studies demonstrate that sound public policy toward futures markets must be based on a thorough understanding of how they function, not on superficial similarities to features of related markets.

In developing this project on the Economics and Regulation of Futures Markets, we consulted extensively with government officials, representatives of the private sector, and academic scholars. These consultations contributed significantly to shaping the character of the studies and reviewing them as they were written. To provide for systematic advice and review while the project was under way, an advisory committee, chaired by Gary L. Seevers, was established. Representatives of the major future exchanges, users of futures services, and research professionals from universities and business firms made up the committee. A research advisory committee was also established to identify issues for examination and to survey research under way by leading scholars. This committee was cochaired by Philip McBride Johnson and William L. Silber. The members of the advisory committees are listed at the back of this book.

The advisory committee met in Washington at the outset of the project to help identify the policy issues that should receive priority, and members or their representatives met jointly with the authors when their studies were planned and drafted. Subsequent meetings were held in New York and Chicago. These committees made invaluable contributions to the research, both through the advice and criticism that they provided and through the access to knowledgeable people in the industry that they made possible.

Although these studies were carried out entirely separately from the government studies, the project benefited from frequent consultation with government agency officials and staff. In particular, Susan M. Phillips, chairperson of the CFTC, members of the CFTC's economics staff, Frederick Struble, associate director of the FRB, and members of the FRB staff provided information to authors and helpful suggestions in response to draft papers.

The assistance of many individuals in preparing and reviewing individual papers is acknowledged in the two major volumes in which the studies are published. I want to take this opportunity to express my thanks not only to those who assisted but also to the authors who prepared the studies and responded to requests for revisions or clarification. In addition, I want especially to thank the chairmen and members of the advisory committees for their support, advice, and assistance throughout the project.

MARVIN H. KOSTERS
Director
Government Regulation Studies

Introduction

In the spring and summer of 1983, the American Enterprise Institute began to assemble a group of scholars and other professionals familiar with the American futures markets to conduct research and to inquire into issues that had emerged in Congress, in the federal regulatory agencies, and in the media concerning the new direction being taken by those markets. As trading volume soared and products with familiar names—including money itself—took center stage, it became increasingly clear that a greater understanding of the futures markets was needed. It was also evident that the newer products might carry with them problems that had not yet been thoroughly explored. Both overt and subtle competitive skirmishes between the securities and futures industries, the Commodity Futures Trading Commission (CFTC) and the Securities and Exchange Commission (SEC), and even the oversight committees in the Congress added a sense of urgency to the process.

The Congress commissioned several studies of the issues, to be carried out by the CFTC, the SEC, and other federal agencies. At the same time, private sector analyses were undertaken, including this AEI project. The eleven papers springing from that effort have now been published in two volumes. Each paper stands on its own merits and yet constitutes part of a broader, interdependent analysis of the futures market. The purpose of this overview is to join together the major policy issues stated or implied in the studies. Many of the issues cut across the spectrum of futures contracts, being relevant both to traditional commodities and to newer financial instruments.

The futures markets have undergone spectacular growth and change in the past decade. The rapid expansion in trading volume is chronicled by Anne E. Peck.[1] From 1970 through 1983 futures volume increased tenfold, from less than 13 million to more than 137 million contracts. Although the newer financial futures accounted for much of the growth, the period also saw remarkable increases for grains and oilseeds (500 percent), livestock (400 percent), and foodstuffs (200 percent). All nonfinancial futures combined accounted for 64 percent of total volume in 1983.

That figure of 64 percent for 1983 was virtually 100 percent only half a decade earlier. The difference was due to the invention and later explosion of financial futures: government obligations, private debt instruments, stock indexes, economic indicators, and foreign currencies. This phenomenon has not only radically altered the complexion of the futures markets. It has also introduced new concepts, such as "cash settlement," that are being tested even in the traditional commodities; contributed to the willingness of Congress and the CFTC to reopen options trading on futures markets; and invoked anxieties in the federal establishment, the regulatory agencies, and the affected industries about the potential implications—even dangers—of these new money-related instruments.

1
Cash Settlement

No single event since the advent of futures trading in the United States has been more significant than the evolution of the technique known as cash settlement. This development, addressed primarily by Allen B. Paul,[2] has permitted futures trading—including risk aversion—in property that cannot efficiently or readily be physically delivered and, indeed, where transfer of the underlying commodity is completely impossible.

As is frequently the case, the law was partly responsible for the late arrival of cash settlement. For decades it was believed (or at least deemed likely) that an instrument would not be considered a futures contract as a matter of law unless it provided for the transfer of actual property from seller to buyer. Indeed, arrangements between parties to settle all claims in cash were frequently viewed as wagers, with criminal as well as moral implications. The breakthrough came in two stages. In 1974 Congress gave the new CFTC "exclusive jurisdiction" over all futures trading, which forced state gambling laws off the stage. It was thereafter the decision solely of the commission whether futures contracts could lawfully be settled in cash. In 1981 the commission answered that question in the affirmative, and in many futures contracts today all obligations are settled in cash.

"Cash settlement," as Paul says, describes not merely a way to conclude futures obligations but the actual prohibition of physical delivery by exchange rules. The only settlement method allowed is cash payment between the parties. While roughly 95 percent of all futures contracts were already settled in cash through a process of offsetting the original contract obligation with an opposite purchase or sale, the new procedure enhanced trading in nondeliverable items by foreclosing either party from any recourse except cash payment.

Aside from the perceived legal barriers mentioned above, cash settlement emerged slowly because the final price must be based on reliable commercial values from sources reasonably protected from tampering (such as manipulation). Otherwise the concluding price of the futures contract might deviate markedly from the true value recognized in commercial channels and thus impair the use of those futures as a price hedge. Similarly, a final settlement price that has relied on manipulated source data will be invalid for hedging purposes and may prove exploitative of speculators as well.

With those caveats in mind, cash settlement has been created for futures on both tangible and intangible items. Potato futures, which encountered repeated problems when physical delivery was required, are now settled in cash. Cash settlement appears to be the only way to resolve futures contracts in economic abstractions, such as the consumer price index or ocean freight rates. And for stock indexes the theoretical possibility of bundling hundreds of securities for physical delivery is outweighed by the cost and inconvenience of doing so under most circumstances, so that cash settlement is more attractive.

Paul notes that some futures contracts are settled in cash against the closing prices of other, larger futures contracts. The danger that settlement prices will not be faithful to commercial values increases when the final pricing of one futures contract relies on prices in another futures market rather than on actual sales in the "cash" market. This pricing mechanism has, however, thus far been confined to so-called minicontracts exactly mirroring (except for smaller size) a more active futures contract traded on another exchange. Because the dominant futures contract is typically subject to physical delivery, its final price and the commercial value tend to converge. The minicontract effectively borrows that convergence. Similarly, where cash settlement applies to the dominant contract and the settlement price is commercially valid, reliance by the minicontract on that price seems unobjectionable.

Futures contracts that are settled in cash have been referred to as a "white-collar numbers game" by skeptical members of the Congress. As William L. Silber points out, however,[3] gambling analogies are inapposite when discussing futures, including their settlement, because the risks addressed by futures are existing perils arising from economic life, not contrived as recreation, as in card games, slot machines, or horse races.

Indeed, cash settlement may actually improve the efficiency of the futures markets by ensuring that cash and futures prices will converge at the contract's expiration. Requiring physical delivery of stock index futures (other examples might also be cited) would be so burdensome that the traditional dynamics for convergence—arbitraging between the cash and futures markets (discussed by Peck)—might not occur and price distortions could result.

Although cash settlement is most often associated with financial futures contracts, such a system already exists for potato futures and is being studied for livestock futures as well. Wayne D. Purcell and

Michael A. Hudson[4] note that the Chicago Mercantile Exchange, long the dominant futures market in cattle and hogs, has modified physical delivery by adopting a transferable certificate system and, more recently, by contemplating a true cash settlement procedure. That a classic agricultural futures market would seek a way to avoid delivery suggests, and Purcell and Hudson find, that producers like cash settlement. Even where physical transfer of property is possible, cash settlement may be preferred in commercial circles as more efficient or convenient.

The greatest policy issue raised by cash settlement is not whether a "numbers game" results or whether the "cash" prices relied on are sufficiently valid or representative to aid hedging. Cash settlement of futures contracts does not convert them into gambling any more than a shareholder's acceptance of cash rather than corporate assets upon sale of his or her stock does. And valuation questions—whether the settlement price is "true"—are commonly resolved in the design process; if they are insoluble, cash settlement is not used. Rather, it is the potential of cash settlement that seems most troubling to some observers. Cash settlement effectively allows trading in anything having a quantifiable value. Or, stated differently, cash settlement makes theoretically possible the hedging of virtually every economic risk. Despite the complexities involved, cash settlement creates the possibility of trading or hedging the abstract value of air fares, rental space, casualty losses, medical services, and even the weather.

The pertinent futures contracts, which would probably be index instruments since most underlying goods or services are far from uniform or fungible, could moderate risks and create speculative opportunities for the first time in areas of society or the economy that may not initially welcome such attention. Like financial futures, which resurrected anxieties generally dissipated for traditional commodities, the notion that futures markets may infiltrate new sectors of the economy will take some getting used to. At the same time, as futures markets extend their reach and become more influential, it will be increasingly vital that futures contracts be designed, traded, and regulated in the best possible way. The challenge will be to facilitate the expansion of the futures markets' risk-management services wherever they can be usefully employed while recognizing that such expansion will amplify injury if the markets do not perform properly.

2
New Products

Cash settlement has changed the mechanics of futures trading in some products. Concurrently, the futures markets have expanded their product lines and, in doing so, have raised the policy issues of whether futures trading in the new areas is appropriate and, if it is, whether those markets provide adequate safeguards against abuse.

Financial Futures

Financial futures markets have expanded the most dramatically of any futures markets in the past decade, a phenomenon addressed principally by Silber but viewed from a congressional and regulatory perspective by Charles M. Seeger.[5] Agricultural futures may have raised public concern because a vital commodity—food—was being traded (see Philip McBride Johnson),[6] but financial futures implicated the "ultimate commodity": money. Money is a temporary substitute for virtually all goods and services. If financial futures were bad, no one could reasonably expect to escape the consequences.

As Silber points out, financial futures were among the first to arise where there were already large, efficient markets in the underlying Treasury securities, foreign currencies, bank instruments, equity stocks, and the like. Far from being redundant, however, financial futures markets, Silber concludes, have offered the benefits of reduced transaction costs and improved market liquidity, lowering the cost of capital to business firms.

These benefits, it appears, were not self-evident in the mid-1970s when financial futures first appeared. The government expressed concerns, as Seeger reports, that highly leveraged financial futures could encourage a cornering of the government securities market, interfere with the Treasury Department's debt management programs, and lure unsophisticated new investors who are (or believe themselves to be) more conversant with a Treasury bill than a pork belly. Finally, since there is no limit to the number of futures contracts that can be created in a particular item, it was feared that financial futures contracts would proliferate and place huge demands on the

Treasury debt securities from traders preparing to deliver on their contracts.

The advent of financial futures triggered a rush by almost all the futures markets to participate in what is correctly perceived as a major new growth area for the industry. This "proliferation" of financial futures has been said to have adverse consequences ranging from excessive pressures on the cash market to a profligate failure rate for new offerings. As Silber points out, most efforts to offer duplicate products have failed, but even so the survivors have enjoyed huge success. The fatality rate brings into question whether futures markets take adequate care to develop products with genuine potential. Similarly, it could be asked whether the trading public should be made to assume not only the risk of adverse prices but also the risk—even the likelihood—that the contract in which they hold positions will wither and die. Finally, brokers have expressed concern that product proliferation forces salespeople to serve customers without proper training and renders product promotion both haphazard and wasteful.

These objections are well known at the Commodity Futures Trading Commission. The commission has traditionally viewed the high failure rate as one might view it in any commercial battle; that is, it should be the right of business to try even if success is remote. In addition, federal law does not require the commission to predict whether a new contract will succeed. The only test is whether the contract can serve an economic purpose at minimum risk of manipulation or price distortion. Even so, Silber suggests that public participants be warned by account executives at brokerage firms that new contracts may fail to survive and may thus cause liquidity problems.

There is little evidence of injury to the public from the demise of a futures contract. Failing health is quickly spotted, and traders tend either to depart before conditions become critical or, if a stronger competitor exists, to shift positions into the more vigorous contract. The risk remains, of course, that advantage might be taken of a dying contract, which may be vulnerable to manipulation because of illiquidity. The commission has adopted regulations to identify, monitor, and if necessary terminate any contract that poses such dangers.

It is desirable for salespeople in the futures industry to know what they are talking about, and it is correct that many are not conversant with a new product until well after its introduction. This is not a problem unique to futures, of course, but applies to the thousands of securities that emerge each year. Indeed, it could be said that new futures pose less of a problem because they have common features and uses, though different underlying items, while each common stock is as unique as the particular company and its management.

With the exception of foreign currency futures, the new financial instruments tend to deal in or relate to securities and therefore invite comparisons of how the futures and securities markets operate and are regulated. Different floor trading systems (see Seymour Smidt) and disparate margining policies, reflecting in part quite different notions of the true purposes of margin controls, exist (see William G. Tomek).[7] In the regulatory arena, other features distinguishing between the securities markets and the futures exchanges are identified in the papers of Seeger and Johnson. Many of the regulations in the securities industry, such as "suitability" rules, have been urged upon the futures markets, in part on an assumption of small, unsophisticated, poorly funded speculators that is not borne out by Dennis W. Draper's research.[8]

Perhaps the most intense focus of concern over financial futures has been whether they will have a negative effect on capital formation in the economy. Aside from occasions when "capital formation" is used as synonymous with the profitability of the securities business (that is, capital formation is "impaired" if business is lost), the main concern seems to be whether financial futures will prove more attractive to investors than placing capital directly into enterprises or whether futures may cause aberrations in securities prices that impede investment in stocks and bonds. Since farmers did not abandon their fields to play the grain futures market a century ago, one might ask why financial futures should threaten the flow of capital to business. Nevertheless, the issue is posed earnestly if not forebodingly.

The entire subject of capital formation and its relation to the financial futures markets is analyzed by Jerome L. Stein.[9] He concludes that the futures markets do not imperil capital formation and may facilitate it by reducing transaction costs, raising the expected return on a portfolio, and diversifying away the systematic risk of securities ownership.

One reason why capital formation issues are raised in connection with financial futures is the affinity between those who might purchase new securities offerings (or help make a secondary market) and those who might find financial futures attractive. Thus, although the existence of cattle futures poses little risk that consumers will stop at their brokerage house instead of at the butcher's, the clientele for products such as stock index futures is similar to that for stocks and bonds (although the latter group is far larger).

Stein notes that a large part of the public's savings is managed by institutions, such as pension funds or insurance companies, and that futures on Treasury instruments and stock indexes improve an institution's expected return for a given level of risk. This benefit and similar benefits realized by others in the chain of securities transactions should contribute positively to capital formation, as both Stein and Silber conclude. Aside from the issues addressed by Stein, the debate over futures versus capital formation presents something of a paradox. In the past it was fashionable in the securities industry to distinguish emphatically between "investing" and "speculating." The former referred to securities customers, the latter to futures traders. Now the same observers express fear that financial futures may entice away their securities clients, an impossibility if the distinction between investing and speculating were as clear as has been alleged. It seems not unreasonable to suggest, therefore, that whatever effect financial futures may have on the capital formation process, they have debunked a bit of semantic sleight of hand.

The evolution of financial futures is noteworthy for at least one additional reason. Because financial futures attracted participation by the economy's most respected and respectable enterprises, the public was forced to revise its previous impression of the futures markets as places frequented only by rowdies and get-rich-quick dreamers. The *crème de la crème* arrived with financial futures, and the industry has not been the same since.

Of particular significance in changing the industry's reputation has been the high public profile of its new users. It was always true that bona fide commercial patronage existed in the futures markets, but those participants were frequently privately held, secretive, publicity-shy enterprises. When it became necessary to offer Congress a glimpse of those commercial users (that is, as hearing witnesses) to prove that the markets were not pure speculative diversions, the firms would often beg off. Today, however, scores of well-known financial institutions appear to be willing and able to come forward as confirmation that responsible people use the financial futures markets.

Commodity Options

Commodity options as now offered on U.S. exchanges involve either a right to sell ("put") or a right to buy ("call") a specific item or a futures contract on that item. In either case the purchaser of the option obtains for a payment ("premium") a limited-time right to complete the transaction at a preagreed price. If it is not profitable to complete the transaction, the option owner may allow it to expire without any further obligation. The seller ("writer") of the option, however, must stand ready to perform whenever the purchaser so desires within the option's life and thus is exposed to the full risk of changes in the product's value. The writer's only compensation is the premium received from the purchaser, which may be insufficient to cover the cost of completing the transaction. Accordingly, options bear risks similar to those of futures contracts for the writer but have attractive limited liability with unlimited profit potential for the purchaser.

Options, which offer the purchaser an opportunity to limit his or her potential losses in ways that futures contracts do not, seem an unlikely target of special "customer protection" debate. Yet they may well be the most highly politicized of all current financial products.

The present regulatory structure mirrors this curious environment. The CFTC came into existence at a time in the mid-1970s when options were either banned entirely (farm products) or were virtually beyond all regulation (everything else). In the latter milieu, as one might expect, a pattern of sharp practices developed as promoters made "sales" of phantom options through outrageous claims and promises. In many instances the promoters represented that the options being sold were those originated on the reputable London commodity exchanges. In fact the buyers received not a true "London option" but merely a hollow commitment from the promoter.

Nevertheless, the code phrase "London option" emerged to describe what was, in fact, American confidence artists fleecing American citizens. Inapposite labels can sometimes take on a life of their own and have an effect on substantive decision making. That is what happened with options. Today, although U.S. markets and some U.S. dealers have been cleared to offer commodity options, foreign exchanges, including those in London, are barred from access to the American public. In at least this respect, regulatory policy fails to recognize that the options scandals of the mid-1970s were not imported from abroad.

Since 1981 most options trading has been confined to designated U.S. contract markets under a federal "pilot program" with special restrictions. It was due to end in October 1985, when the special limitations were expected to be lifted and options trading to be conducted under normal regulatory policies. The commission has announced, however, that it will not take that step and that the pilot program system will continue indefinitely. After three years of near-perfect behavior, options trading evidently remains too hot a subject on Capitol Hill, at the commission, or among the public for definitive decisions to be made.

Options have also been near the center of a jurisdictional controversy between the commission and the Securities and Exchange Commission. Until December 1981, when the two agencies agreed on a division of jurisdiction over options, a running battle had prevented either agency from authorizing trading in what were then gray areas of jurisdiction. Today the futures markets and the securities exchanges trade a wide variety of options, and the two federal agencies administer their roles in relative harmony.

Options trading in this new, moderately more hospitable environment is the subject of the paper by Hans R. Stoll and Robert E. Whaley.[10] In light of the sales abuses that attended options marketing in earlier years, the conclusions of Stoll and Whaley that options are both economically and socially salutary will be weighed by policy makers against any potential resurgence of fraud. The major objections to commodity options are the same as those leveled at financial futures: options are "gambling"; they may prey upon the unsuitable investor; they may distort "cash" prices or divert risk-taking capital from more "productive" uses. Although these concerns will probably generally be answered in the same way as for futures, it remains to be seen whether options will attract a less affluent, more vulnerable investor than futures and, if so, whether at least their sales practices and public access to the options markets should be regulated differently from futures.

3
The "Level Playing Field"

There are many reasons to examine the futures markets and the governmental policies affecting them. We might wish simply to understand the system better or to test whether it is as efficient as possible. But candor requires it to be noted that much of the debate over the futures markets, especially since the advent of financial futures, has resulted from apprehension in the futures and securities industries that the other enjoys a competitive advantage by reason of a less strict regulatory environment.

The papers constituting the AEI project focus on many issues that emerged first (or at least most recently) in competitive skirmishes between the futures and securities industries. Customer suitability rules in securities but not in futures might seem to tie one arm behind the securities industry's back. The arduous "economic purpose" analysis of every new futures contract by the Commodity Futures Trading Commission while clearance of new products by the Securities and Exchange Commission is usually quick and simple would appear to give the securities markets a large head start in competition with the futures industry for similar products. The controversy over whether futures margins are too low when contrasted with securities margins is, at heart, a plea for regulatory neutrality in matters having competitive significance.

The rivalry between the futures and securities industries did not become acute so long as those markets confined their activities to traditional areas—physical commodities for futures and trade in stocks and bonds for the securities exchanges. The tension has surfaced, rather, because the securities industry created futures-like instruments traded as securities options on the central markets and the futures markets introduced contracts on various securities or securities indexes. Through securities options the stock exchanges have created products that are not means to create capital, as common stocks or corporate bonds are, but can be used as insulation against adverse price changes. As Stoll and Whaley note, "Options are primarily a means of shifting risk, not of shifting capital."

Seeger and Johnson discuss in detail the issues that have arisen as each industry grows increasingly concerned that its regulation—the futures markets by the CFTC and the securities options exchanges by the SEC—may skew the competitive environment in favor of the other. The perception that CFTC policies fail adequately to protect the small trader is questioned, however, by Draper, who finds that avocational traders have considerable affluence and experience in trading markets. Conversely, the view of the securities industry that its options are stifled by harsh SEC policies is receding as the SEC modifies its rules in such areas as margins to reflect the difference between options and the true securities under its jurisdiction.

Floor trading procedures (for example, specialists versus the floor "crowd") and related regulatory policies respecting execution of transactions (for example, "side-by-side" trading) in both the futures and the securities markets are also cited as having possible competitive significance. Smidt recounts the significant differences between where and how transactions are conducted, as well as the legal and regulatory backdrop that has evolved in each industry to accommodate and monitor its trading environment. Smidt also observes, with regard to competing products, that disparate regulatory policies between futures and securities might be harmonized in several ways, including replacement of current divisions based on product identification with a system of agency assignment along functional lines. Each agency would then oversee and set standards for the function or functions assigned to it.

Smidt illustrates the concept of functional regulation by distinguishing, for example, between securities issuers that originate the investment, brokerage firms that promote and sell it to the general public, and exchanges where buyers and sellers may gather to trade it. Another approach to functional regulation is related not to what the regulated persons do but rather to what the products themselves are designed to achieve. This is, in fact, the method of analysis that accounts in significant measure for why futures regulation and securities regulation are in certain respects quite different.

Regulation according to product function would presumably begin by identifying the economic role or "purpose" of the product. If the product were merely a wagering vehicle that served no other role in the economy, it could, if lawful, be assigned to public agencies that oversee gaming programs. If the product raised or helped to raise capital, it could be regulated by agencies that are expert in such areas—the SEC and the various state securities administrators. If the principal economic purpose were to transfer price risks, an agency—now the CFTC—would be made responsible for monitoring that service.

The jurisdictional accord entered into by the CFTC and the SEC in 1981 is partly (but only partly) built on the concept of functional regulation. It follows that theme by giving the CFTC complete and absolute jurisdiction over all futures contracts and options on futures, both of which are recognized hedging instruments. It deviates from a purely functional analysis in other aspects, however, such as the retention by the SEC of sole federal jurisdiction over options directly on securities that do not raise or help raise capital except in a highly indirect way but do appear to provide some forms of hedging protection. For options on foreign currencies, the accord authorizes the SEC to act under certain circumstances even though foreign currencies are not securities and do not promote capital formation (although options on them could be a means of hedging).

The idiosyncrasies of the accord when tested strictly against a functional standard are concessions to real world forces. No agreement could have been reached between the CFTC and the SEC if major sacrifices of preexisting jurisdiction had been demanded by either side. It does not follow, however, that the goal is unworthy. Within the boundaries set by politics or pragmatism, it may still be desirable for regulatory programs to be catalogued according to the principal economic role of a particular product, rather than whether it is called a security or a commodity. As Smidt points out, trading floor practices and regulation in futures and securities markets differ in part because those markets do not have precisely the same function to perform. Since "functional" distinctions already play a part in how regulatory policy is made, it is a relatively short step beyond that to examine jurisdictional boundaries in the same way.

4
The Margin Debate

It is not evident why futures margins should provoke the intensity or frequency of debate that they do. By any measure they have provided excellent financial protection for the futures markets. Peck notes, for example, that futures margins combined with daily marking of positions to the market have reduced the risk of contract default virtually to zero. The concerns appear to come from other directions, some of them competitive (the "level playing field") and some of them governmental, where change (almost always meaning higher margins) is sought for purposes unrelated or only remotely and inadvertently related to the financial integrity of the system.

Tomek addresses these issues by explaining what margins are ("performance bonds"), how they differ from their namesake in the securities world, and how they are established and administered. He also discusses the intended purpose of the margins and whether that purpose is met or is the correct focus. Stoll and Whaley and Johnson observe, however, that exchange-traded securities options and futures contracts have more characteristics in common than futures and traditional stocks and bonds. Implicitly, one might expect that margins for futures and securities options would be more similar, although continuing differences (such as federal insurance for securities accounts) create a somewhat different credit-risk equation.

The securities industry has expressed anxiety that futures margins are low and that, where securities products must compete for the same patronage, the futures markets have an undue and unfair advantage. It is true, of course, that futures margins are usually small, at least when compared with the full market value of the item underlying the futures contract. But the margin does not purchase the underlying item or any part of it. A securities investor who places $5,000 to buy a $10,000 stock is half-owner of the securities; the futures trader who places $500 on a $10,000 contract has acquired nothing but the right, on delivery of the underlying item, to pay the full $10,000 purchase price. Moreover, futures margins are payable by the seller as well as by the buyer, underscoring the performance bond purpose of the deposit. One might reasonably question whether futures margins, paid by both sides even though neither title nor cash passes between them, can seduce the investing public away from the securities markets. (Even in options, as Stoll and Whaley observe, the seller receives compensation immediately in the form of a premium from the option buyer, but the futures seller receives nothing at that time.)

Another nonfinancial purpose sometimes suggested for futures margins is as a drawbridge, to be raised against the unwary or unsuited or to dampen "excessive speculation," as Stoll and Whaley point out. Tomek discusses the potential use of margins to affect trading volume, open interest, or price behavior. Whether these uses of margins, even if feasible, would be appealing or offensive depends on one's attitude toward using prices to control consumer habits. Futures margins have not generally been employed in those ways, and Tomek concludes that margin policy may be a poor instrument to achieve those goals. Moreover, there might be legitimate grounds for worry that, if margins are allowed to function for those purposes, they might also be used to manipulate market prices or to force rivals from the market. "Social goals" leave far more room for mischief than a system based on such measurable, objective factors as market risk.

Another criticism of low futures margins is that they permit the control of substantial value at minimal cost. The futures margin, usually about 5 percent of the underlying commodity's face value, provides a 20-to-1 leverage. In some quarters it is evidently considered disturbing that wealth can be controlled with so small an investment. Suffice it to say that futures are not the only economic activity with such a feature. If it were deemed unlawful or socially repugnant to capture a large value for a fraction of its full cost, there would be few homeowners in America today.

5
The Nonprice Benefits of Futures

Much has been written over the years about the role of futures markets in forecasting prices, discovering values, and hedging commercial risks. Silber emphasizes the improved liquidity provided by futures markets even when well-developed cash markets exist.[11] Peck examines these issues as well as another important service provided by the futures markets—the ability to plan ahead. This last economic benefit is somewhat difficult to quantify because it is not often readily observable. The decisions whether to plan or produce, lend or borrow, invest or abstain, and if so when and how much, usually occur behind closed doors. Even so, it is extremely valuable to recognize that a futures contract on, say, soybeans or stock indexes buys not only a right to the underlying item but also time.

Futures allow decisions to be postponed. Stated more dramatically, futures avert panic by reducing the risk of loss if a decision is deferred until tomorrow or next month. Futures constitute a kind of prebuying or preselling through which it is possible to lock in a price without immediately carrying out the transaction.

Peck relates this phenomenon principally to the "hard" commodity arena, where it has enjoyed great success, but indicates that it has applications in financial instruments as well. Silber likewise notes the value of futures "to those dealing in the cash commodity who need prices to plan production and consumption decisions," and Stein cites the use of futures to lock in a price before funds for actual purchase become available. The value of futures in making forward planning decisions, even if a market position is not taken, is discussed by Purcell and Hudson. Similarly, a decision whether to purchase or sell a common stock can be delayed more easily if stock index futures are acquired to eliminate the systematic risk of stock market change in the interim. Borrowing can be deferred with less risk of interest rate increases if financial futures are held during the intervening period. In other words, the decision maker has more time to make up his or her mind, which means more time for exploring other alternatives or for conditions to become more favorable.

Corporate acquisitions or buy-outs illustrate this benefit of financial futures. During takeovers two enormous risks are often paired: first, the danger that the funds borrowed to finance the venture (often at floating rates) will rise in cost to the point where the debt burden proves so crippling that the campaign must be abandoned; second, the risk that the securities being bought up to attain control will depreciate in value, either during their accumulation or immediately thereafter. Either of these contingencies could thwart the objective, by discouraging financial backing at the outset or by becoming problems in midstream. To some degree a well-conceived financial futures position can cushion the effects of rising interest rates on the venture's borrowings, and stock index futures can moderate the effects of marketwide trends affecting the price of the acquired common stock. Neither strategy is likely to be a perfect shelter, but it will at least slow the rate of losses (that is, the rise in cost) enough to buy more time than would otherwise be available to reassess and regroup.

A buy-out typically takes the form of "going private" through repurchase of shares from public stockholders. It poses many of the same risks as a takeover. Heavy borrowing is usually needed, which may be at floating rates as well. Financial futures can act as shock absorbers in the event that borrowing costs rise and thereby permit the acquiring parties (such as inside management) more time to complete the buy-out.

Another benefit of futures hedging in the context of financial dealings is what might be called the "prudence factor." In takeovers and buy-outs, for example, a successful effort often results in substantial new debts or other liabilities for the company. This would occur, for instance, if the debt incurred during the takeover or buy-out were transferred to the acquired entity. A dramatic and negative change in the organization's balance sheet or financial condition might be viewed in some quarters as irresponsible, especially if minority shareholders remained who must help to carry the new burden. Hedging in the futures markets would constitute an effort by the new management to minimize those effects and thus to demonstrate concern for the interests of all the shareholders.

The foregoing illustrations are somewhat hypothetical. Extensive research would be needed to determine whether they are feasible strategies in particular circumstances. Nevertheless, they help to focus on two seldom-mentioned benefits of futures hedging: acquiring extra time, and therefore flexibility, for decision making; and maintaining a reputation as responsible, prudent managers.

6
Futures in Live or Perishable Commodities

Silber characterizes most financial instruments as "perfectly storable commodities." Not all innovation in the past decade has been limited, however, to those products. On the contrary, Purcell and Hudson examine creative new answers to what may be the least storable of all commodities: live animals.

Well within my memory the futures industry considered the creation of a futures contract on any perishable commodity impossible. The item might spoil; if alive, it might sicken or even die. It was not storable in the same way as corn or metals, and production could take place year-round. As Purcell and Hudson explain, those obstacles were overcome by what is clearly one of the best examples of contract adaptation in the history of the futures markets. The advent of financial futures can be credited in no small measure to the success of seemingly impossible commodity futures, which led the industry to believe that anything might be possible.

Farm commodities like cattle are particularly sensitive to criticism. Farmers are well organized and not timid in expressing their opinions. Significantly, the futures markets fall within the congressional jurisdiction of the House and Senate Agriculture committees, which would not dare to ignore their farm constituencies. As Purcell and Hudson recount, however, livestock futures tend to reduce the variability of prices in the cash market as compared with periods when futures have not been traded and interact with rather than dominate the cash market.

A major problem in the livestock markets appears to be a lack of understanding about how futures should be used for maximum protection. Purcell and Hudson explain that producers watch livestock futures prices and often make planning decisions on the assumption that those predictions will remain valid throughout the intervening period. That assumption can be quite wrong, because of the ease with which production can be increased in response to bullish price predictions, thus applying downward pressure not accounted for in the initial futures price. To maintain the validity of the original decision, producers would need to—but infrequently do—take hedge positions in the futures market. To the extent that hedging may be unattractive to producers because of physical delivery, the shift to cash settlement systems that Purcell and Hudson think possible might prove salutary.

Livestock futures have been traded for roughly twenty years and yet are repeatedly singled out in Congress and by agricultural groups as suspect or at least troublesome. Purcell and Hudson correctly point to misunderstanding of the markets, even after two decades of operation. As the futures industry continues its vigorous expansion into new fields and adds to its traditional complement of commodities, the experience of the livestock futures markets should be remembered. In particular, the indispensable value of effective education in the use of futures should not be overlooked.

7
The Dynamics of Regulation

Johnson and Seeger compare major regulatory policies governing the securities and futures industries, and their simplified conclusion is that each scheme works reasonably well in its own environment. They also try to show that the debate between the CFTC and the SEC has sometimes been driven by competitive fear and jurisdictional greed as well as by public policy concerns.

Although considerable tension has existed between the investment community and its regulators, Seeger notes that the markets and their government overseers have a number of common objectives: market integrity, competitive pricing, and commercial freedom. Interplay between the two forces can help to draw attention to problems and to work toward solutions, as Purcell and Hudson's chronology of recent changes in the cattle futures contracts illustrates. As Tomek points out for margin setting, however, government decision making is sometimes a poor substitute for private initiative, even when a common objective is sought.

This notion of the limits of regulatory power is further discussed by Johnson, who observes that regulation is a highly specialized form of governmental activity. It can work well—even superbly—in moderating excesses in legitimate industries because those who are subject to regulation will not risk their right to remain in business. Regulation is ill-suited, however, to catching swindlers who neither expect nor intend to be in business for more than a short time.

For regulators to profess an ability to perform criminal law enforcement tasks is dangerous enough because of the assured failure of that effort, but it is doubly damaging because the public will not tolerate failure by a regulator. Police, judges, and jailers are forgiven their inability to forestall all crime, but the public believes that regulators exist to prevent harm before it can occur. There is no shorter or surer route to public contempt than for a regulator to promise what cannot be reliably delivered. This fact is too often overlooked by regulators, including the CFTC.

8
Final Note: Playing to Strength

In expanding and clarifying an understanding of the futures markets, the AEI studies meet any "value-added" test that might be applied. They examine many fundamentals of futures—key elements of how the markets function and whether trading activity is conducted and regulated sensibly. Some issues are old wine in new bottles (for example, margins) as futures expand into new areas and thereby assemble different questioners with the same traditional concerns. Other issues tenaciously adhere to futures markets of long standing, such as the debate over the efficacy of livestock futures trading.

I find it difficult to read the AEI papers without wondering. I wonder why it is that the same "concerns" about futures are voiced generation after generation; why reasonably understandable concepts like futures "margins" must be explained ad nauseam; why concluding a futures transaction through cash payment is controversial although securities are nearly always closed out in exactly the same way; and why a populist approach to futures regulation (identified by Draper and by Johnson) has not withered under the evidence that speculation in these markets by nonprofessionals is largely a country club sport.

The authors of the AEI papers, like those who have sought under other banners to educate and inform about futures, are unlikely to attract the general public as readers. Draper as well as other researchers tells us that the consuming public remain virtual strangers to the futures markets, with minor exceptions that would hardly justify the toil. Unless the public's silent boycott of the futures markets can somehow be broken, their attitudes or prejudices toward futures will probably remain the same. As busy and beleaguered visitors to this planet, we learn what we need to know, and futures, like foreign languages, are not on most Americans' lists.

The AEI studies and other companion efforts should, however, bear fruit in two locations—government policy making and industry planning. The AEI papers send useful messages to government policy makers. Accordingly, the audience for my closing remarks will be the industry's planners, those who must decide the direction of the futures markets for the next generation or so.

Let us begin with certain facts. The futures markets in the United States have existed for nearly as long as the domestic securities exchanges. Both industries have actively promoted their wares to the general public for well over a century. Today the securities markets boast some 43 million stockholders, while the number of nonprofessional futures speculators is seldom placed above 200,000—one-half of 1 percent.

Why? Promotional efforts in the futures industry have been persistent and often ingenious. Exchanges and brokerage firms scour the nation for potential traders, and futures can be ordered from many hundreds of local offices. The daily newspapers bristle with advertisements bringing futures as close to American citizens as the telephone. Even so, the chasm between patronage of securities and of futures remains huge.

The culprit appears to be what I will call the "fundamental meanness" of speculative futures trading. Although futures contracts as risk-shifting (hedging) vehicles appeal greatly to commercial enterprises, speculative futures trading is a fast-paced, high-risk exercise for people who are not professional traders. The 20-to-1 leverage typically available through futures causes losses as surely as gains to multiply at phenomenal speed. The daily mark-to-market system means that setbacks must be remedied in real funds—and immediately. Moreover, the specter of being required to deliver or accept an unfamiliar and usually unwanted commodity is chilling for most people. Finally, the burden of closely and continuously monitoring market developments is beyond the capacity of most investors. All these factors conspire against broad public participation in the futures markets.

In certain ways the futures markets already acknowledge this problem. The "commodity pool," for example, has evolved to offer the general public a more attractive way to participate in futures trading. The funds of many contributors are combined into a unified trading program allowing larger and more diversified holdings. More important, each participant is guaranteed against losing more than the initial contribution; no personal margin calls are issued to participants; deliveries, if any, are made or taken by the pool rather than by individual participants; and the entire enterprise is handled by professional managers. In effect, the public is offered the equivalent of a passive security with limited risk and none of the burdens of maintaining a direct account in the futures market.

The speculative population of the futures markets today consists of small subsets of the public: full-time professional traders, many of them members of the exchanges or operators of pools; comparatively few affluent avocational participants; and commercial enterprises that, in addition to hedging, may engage in outright trading and arbitrage. Thus far, at least, these speculators appear adequate in number and capital to perform a market-making function and facilitate hedging.

On the other side of the ledger are commercial enterprises using futures to shift away from themselves certain price risks associated with dealing in the underlying product. This group is heavily courted by the futures industry as well, but the promotion of hedging is generally viewed as quite separate from the campaign to enlist the general public as speculators.

The failing of the futures industry has been not its objective but its means. The general public is indeed a vast market, as the securities industry has demonstrated. But it has not responded positively to the futures industry's principal strategy: soliciting speculative trading accounts. The public at large is saying no to speculative ventures and, conversely, is implying a preference for greater stability and safety. A new strategy responsive to the public's needs and yet furthering futures trading is called for.

For many goods or services in today's retail economy the consumer is denied price certainty. Price volatility has caused originators and vendors to shift pricing risks to the ultimate consumer. Fixed-rate borrowing is no longer available to most Americans because lenders refuse to deal with interest rate gyrations. Automobile insurance costs change as frequently as every six months because insurers have similar fears of uncontrollable costs. In export transactions sellers often insist that payment be made in their nation's currency to avoid adverse exchange rate fluctuations. Many if not most of these efforts to shift price risk from vendor to consumer are due to the absence of an efficient, economical means for the merchant to hedge that risk.

The highly successful hedging services provided by futures markets could become an avenue to remedy this problem facing the general public, not by making them individual hedgers or speculators but by creating new fixed-price consumer goods and services that will probably be hedged in futures by vendors. It is not inevitable that most home mortgages today are placed at variable interest rates or that casualty insurance, air transportation, residential apartment space, and many other recurring consumer needs are characterized by the high frequency with which prices are revised (usually adversely to the consumer).

These offerings could be made more marketable to a broader audience if their prices were stabilized or their durations extended. For vendors to relieve consumers of price risk, they must either embrace that risk or find another way to pass on the risk to others. The futures market is one way to transfer that risk. As sales increase in the newly price-safe products, futures trading by vendors should increase as well.

The opportunity exists for a genuine research-and-development partnership between the futures markets and commercial enterprises where variable-rate products and services may be converted into fixed-price items by coordinated action in the two sectors: creation of new consumer products (or services) and futures that directly complement each other. This would be a departure from past practice in the futures industry, which has generally responded to independent commercial trends. Here both the consumer product and its companion futures contract would emerge from the same process.

To be feasible, this joint effort would require the development of fairly uniform consumer products. Since futures contracts have standardized terms, so must the hedged product. Moreover, the futures contract must be actively traded to offer efficient, readily available hedging. Accordingly, the new consumer products cannot have widely disparate features precluding a price-trend correlation with the futures contract or have so small a consumer market that the futures contract trades thinly. To avoid these pitfalls, the futures exchanges must play an active role from the start in creating the new fixed-price consumer items, something that they have not done before to any significant degree.

Conversely, it would be necessary to reassess existing futures contracts, as well as create new contracts, to ensure the highest possible correlation with the new family of consumer products. The overall result of this process could be consumer products more attractive than existing offerings and futures contracts that are excellent hedges for those products. For example, both a new form of fixed-rate mortgage and a new interest rate futures contract might emerge.

If such an initiative were undertaken by the futures industry on a broad and continuing scale, the appeal of fixed-price products or services should generate greater demand among consumers. If the new consumer products were widely accepted by the general public, the futures volume generated by hedging those sales might be spectacular. The futures industry would enjoy the same increase in volume as if it had done what now appears impossible—persuaded the general public to participate directly. This concept is not new. More than a century ago grain merchants developed the forward contract, which guaranteed farmers a price for their next harvest while generating fresh futures volume as the merchants hedge those commitments. That principle, however, has not been applied to other areas in any consistent or systematic way.

The regulatory implications of this marketing strategy are also quite positive. The futures industry's historical efforts to solicit direct public speculation have given a consumer-protection slant to regulation, such as a demand for higher margins or for suitability rules to keep the little guy out. The new sales focus on commercial vendors and the better, safer consumer products that would flow from this approach should reduce government concerns and enhance the industry's reputation.

Public speculation will continue, of course, as in the past. Nothing suggested here would impede trading in the futures markets by any person so inclined. We know, however, that avocational speculators are relatively few and well-to-do. We also observe that the general public does not participate. Under these circumstances the public must be reached in another way, one that does not endanger the regulatory environment. What I offer here is a thought on how to add significant growth to the futures markets by indirect contact with the public and improve the regulatory climate at the same time.

Notes

1. Anne E. Peck, "The Economic Role of Traditional Commodity Futures Markets," in Anne E. Peck, ed., *Futures Markets: Their Economic Role* (Washington, D.C.: American Enterprise Institute, 1985), pp. 1–81.
2. See Allen B. Paul, "The Role of Cash Settlement in Futures Contract Specifications," in Anne E. Peck, ed., *Futures Markets: Regulatory Issues* (Washington, D.C.: American Enterprise Institute, 1985), pp. 271–328.
3. William L. Silber, "The Economic Role of Financial Futures," in Peck, *Futures Markets: Their Economic Role*, pp. 83–114.
4. Wayne D. Purcell and Michael A. Hudson, "The Economic Roles and Implications of Trade in Livestock Futures," in Peck, *Futures Markets: Regulatory Issues*, pp. 329–76.
5. Charles M. Seeger, "The Development of Congressional Concern about Financial Futures Markets," in Peck, *Futures Markets: Regulatory Issues*, pp. 1–47.
6. Philip McBride Johnson, "Federal Regulations in Securities and Futures Markets," in Peck, *Futures Markets: Their Economic Role*, pp. 291–325.
7. Seymour Smidt, "Trading Floor Practices on Futures and Securities Exchanges: Economics, Regulation, and Policy Issues," and William G. Tomek, "Margins on Futures Contracts: Their Economic Roles and Regulation," in Peck, *Futures Markets: Regulatory Issues*, pp. 49–142, 143–209.
8. Dennis W. Draper, "The Small Public Trader in Futures Markets," in Peck, *Futures Markets: Regulatory Issues*, pp. 211–69.
9. Jerome L. Stein, "Futures Markets and Capital Formation," in Peck, *Futures Markets: Their Economic Role*, pp. 115–204.
10. Hans R. Stoll and Robert E. Whaley, "The New Option Markets," in Peck, *Futures Markets: Their Economic Role*, pp. 205–89.
11. The contribution of futures markets to improved liquidity is also emphasized in Joseph M. Burns, *A Treatise on Markets: Spot, Futures, and Options* (Washington, D.C.: American Enterprise Institute, 1979).

Contributors

Project on the Economics and Regulation of Futures Markets

DENNIS W. DRAPER is an associate professor of finance in the Graduate School of Business, University of Southern California, Los Angeles.

MICHAEL A. HUDSON is an assistant professor of agricultural economics in the Department of Agricultural Economics, University of Illinois at Urbana-Champaign.

PHILIP MCBRIDE JOHNSON is a partner in the law firm of Skadden, Arps, Slate, Meagher & Flom in New York and former chairman of the Commodity Futures Trading Commission.

ALLEN B. PAUL is a former senior economist with the Economic Research Service, U.S. Department of Agriculture, Washington, D.C.

ANNE E. PECK is an associate professor in the Food Research Institute at Stanford University, Stanford, California, and a resident fellow at the American Enterprise Institute while serving as director of the project on the Economics and Regulation of Futures Markets.

WAYNE D. PURCELL is a professor of agricultural economics in the Department of Agricultural Economics, Virginia Polytechnic Institute and State University, Blacksburg, Virginia.

CHARLES M. SEEGER is a partner in the law firm of Neill, Mullenholz, Shaw and Seeger, Washington, D.C.

WILLIAM L. SILBER is a professor of economics and finance in the Graduate School of Business, New York University, New York, New York.

SEYMOUR SMIDT is the Nicholas H. Noyes Professor of Economics and Finance in the Graduate School of Management, Cornell University, Ithaca, New York.

JEROME L. STEIN is the Eastman Professor of Political Economy in the Department of Economics, Brown University, Providence, Rhode Island.

HANS R. STOLL is the Anne Marie and Thomas B. Walker, Jr., Professor of Finance in the Owen Graduate School of Management, Vanderbilt University, Nashville, Tennessee.

WILLIAM G. TOMEK is a professor of agricultural economics in the New York State School of Agriculture and Life Sciences, Cornell University, Ithaca, New York.

ROBERT E. WHALEY is an associate professor of finance in the Department of Finance and Management Science, University of Alberta, Edmonton, Canada.

Project on the Economics and Regulation of Futures Markets

Advisory Committee

Gary L. Seevers (chairman)
Vice-President, Futures Services Department
Goldman, Sachs, and Company

Fred Arditti
President, GNP Commodities

William Brodsky
President, Chicago Mercantile Exchange

Alan Brody
President, Commodity Exchange, Inc.

John J. Conheeny
Chairman, Merrill Lynch Commodities, Inc.

Bennett J. Corn
President, Coffee, Sugar, and Cocoa Exchange, Inc.

Franklin Edwards
Director, Columbia Futures Center
Graduate School of Business, Columbia University

Hendrik Houthakker
Henry Lee Professor of Economics
Department of Economics, Harvard University

Leo Melamed
Chairman, Dellsher Investment Co.

Mark Powers
President, Powers Research Inc.

Irving Redel
President, Redel Trading Company, Inc.

Richard Sandor
Senior Vice-President, Drexel Burnham Lambert

(continued)

Robert K. Wilmouth
President, National Futures Association

Clayton Yeutter
U.S. Trade Representative
Office of the U.S. Trade Representative

Richard Zecher
Chief Economist and Senior Vice-President
Chase Manhattan Bank

Research Advisory Committee

Phillip Cagan
Visiting Scholar
American Enterprise Institute for Public Policy Research

Philip McBride Johnson (cochairman)
Partner
Skadden, Arps, Slate, Meagher & Flom

Paul MacAvoy
Dean, Graduate School of Management
University of Rochester

Anne E. Peck
Associate Professor, Food Research Institute
Stanford University

Charles M. Seeger
Partner
Neill, Mullenholz, Shaw and Seeger

Gary L. Seevers
Vice-President, Futures Services Department
Goldman, Sachs, and Company

William L. Silber (cochairman)
Professor, Graduate School of Business
New York University

See also the companion volume:

Futures Markets:
Their Economic Role

1   THE ECONOMIC ROLE OF TRADITIONAL COMMODITY FUTURES MARKETS
Anne E. Peck

2   THE ECONOMIC ROLE OF FINANCIAL FUTURES
William L. Silber

3   FUTURES MARKETS AND CAPITAL FORMATION
Jerome L. Stein

4   THE NEW OPTION MARKETS
Hans R. Stoll and Robert E. Whaley

5   FEDERAL REGULATION IN SECURITIES AND FUTURES MARKETS
Philip McBride Johnson

325 pp. / 1985 / $21.95

See also the companion volume:

Futures Markets: Regulatory Issues

1. THE DEVELOPMENT OF CONGRESSIONAL CONCERN ABOUT FINANCIAL FUTURES MARKETS *Charles M. Seeger*

2. TRADING FLOOR PRACTICES ON FUTURES AND SECURITIES EXCHANGES: ECONOMICS, REGULATION, AND POLICY ISSUES *Seymour Smidt*

3. MARGINS ON FUTURES CONTRACTS: THEIR ECONOMIC ROLES AND REGULATION *William G. Tomek*

4. THE SMALL PUBLIC TRADER IN FUTURES MARKETS *Dennis W. Draper*

5. THE ROLE OF CASH SETTLEMENT IN FUTURES CONTRACT SPECIFICATION *Allen B. Paul*

6. THE ECONOMIC ROLES AND IMPLICATIONS OF TRADE IN LIVESTOCK FUTURES *Wayne D. Purcell and Michael A. Hudson*

376 pp. / 1985 / $24.95

Selected AEI Publications

A Treatise on Markets: Spot, Futures, and Options, Joseph M. Burns (1979, 145 pp., $5.25)

The Political Economy of Deregulation: Interest Groups in the Regulatory Process, Roger G. Noll and Bruce M. Owens (1983, 164 pp., paper $7.95, cloth $15.95)

The Natural Gas Revolution of 1985, Stephen F. Williams (1985, 48 pp., $5.95)

The Deregulation of Natural Gas, Edward J. Mitchell, ed. (1983, 163 pp., paper $7.95, cloth $15.95)

Essays in Contemporary Economic Problems, 1986: The Impact of the Reagan Program, Phillip Cagan, ed. (1986, about 370 pp., paper $10.95, cloth $19.95)

Incentives vs. Controls in Health Policy: Broadening the Debate, Jack A. Meyer, ed. (1985, 156 pp., paper $7.95, cloth $15.95)

Regulating Consumer Product Safety, W. Kip Viscusi (1984, 116 pp., paper $5.95, cloth $14.95)

The AEI Economist, Herbert Stein, ed., published monthly (one year, $24; single copy, $2.50)

- *Mail orders for publications to:* AMERICAN ENTERPRISE INSTITUTE, 1150 Seventeenth Street, N.W., Washington, D.C. 20036 • *For postage and handling, add 10 percent of total; minimum charge $2, maximum $10 (no charge on prepaid orders)* • *For information on orders, or to expedite service, call toll free 800-424-2873 (in Washington, D.C., 202-862-5869)* • *Prices subject to change without notice.* • *Payable in U.S. currency through U.S. banks only*

AEI Associates Program

The American Enterprise Institute invites your participation in the competition of ideas through its AEI Associates Program. This program has two objectives: (1) to extend public familiarity with contemporary issues; and (2) to increase research on these issues and disseminate the results to policy makers, the academic community, journalists, and others who help shape public policies. The areas studied by AEI include Economic Policy, Education Policy, Energy Policy, Fiscal Policy, Government Regulation, Health Policy, International Programs, Legal Policy, National Defense Studies, Political and Social Processes, and Religion, Philosophy, and Public Policy. For the $49 annual fee, Associates receive
- a subscription to *Memorandum*, the newsletter on all AEI activities
- the AEI publications catalog and all supplements
- a 30 percent discount on all AEI books
- a 40 percent discount for certain seminars on key issues
- subscriptions to any two of the following publications: *Public Opinion*, a bimonthly magazine exploring trends and implications of public opinion on social and public policy questions; *Regulation*, a bimonthly journal examining all aspects of government regulation of society; and *AEI Economist*, a monthly newsletter analyzing current economic issues and evaluating future trends (or for all three publications, send an additional $12).

Call 202/862-7170 or write: AMERICAN ENTERPRISE INSTITUTE
1150 Seventeenth Street, N.W., Suite 301, Washington, D.C. 20036

Davidson College Library

Futures Markets
An Overview of the AEI Studies
Philip McBride Johnson

Drawing on his experience as chairman of the Commodity Futures Trading Commission, the author shows how careful analysis provides insights relevant to current policy concerns, then puts forward his own ideas about them. His overview and policy discussion are based on a series of AEI studies of futures markets, published in two volumes—*Futures Markets: Their Economic Role* and *Futures Markets: Regulatory Issues*, edited by Anne E. Peck.

Philip McBride Johnson is a partner in the law firm of Skadden, Arps, Slate, Meagher & Flom in New York, author of the two-volume legal treatise *Commodities Regulation* (Little, Brown and Company, 1982), and former chairman of the Commodity Futures Trading Commission.

The AEI study is a significant contribution to the developing literature on law and economics. . . . Not only will this study contribute to the general economic theory of futures markets, but it will also provide a conceptual framework which both practitioners and policy makers can use to formulate decisions relating to this dynamic and growing field of economic risk management.

Susan M. Phillips
Chairman, Commodity Futures Trading Commission

Given the depth of information about futures trading, why is it largely ignored by the public? Johnson concludes that the industry has been going about it in the wrong way. He suggests the creation of "new fixed-price consumer goods and services that will probably be hedged in futures by vendors" and adds that acceptance of these new products could generate spectacular volume. We think Mr. Johnson's idea has merit, and we're betting that the innovators in our industry are looking into it.

John Damgard
President, Futures Industry Association

American Enterprise Institute for Public Policy Research
1150 Seventeenth Street, N.W., Washington, D.C. 20036